For free worksheets and activity ideas for this book, please go to

bookconnect.review/dp/worksheetsannunciation

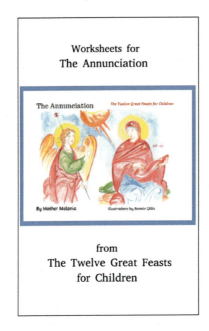

Looking for Pascha (Easter) books?

Pascha at the Duck Pond -

A whimsical look at how to prepare and how NOT to prepare for Pascha.

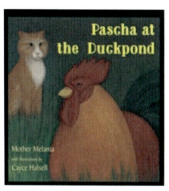

Pascha, the Feast of Feasts
from *The Three-Day Pascha series*

Be glad today! Be glad! Rejoice!
With all creation, lift your voice,
For Christ has died, but lives again –
Restoring life to fallen men.

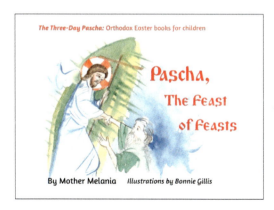

The Annunciation
from *The Twelve Great Feasts for Children*

ISBN 978-1-946991-22-5
Poems © copyright 2003 by Mother Melania (Sister Elayne)
Illustrations © copyright 2003 by Bonnie Gillis

All rights reserved.

Published by Holy Assumption Monastery
1519 Washington St.
Calistoga, CA 94515

Phone: (707) 942-6244
Website: https://holyassumptionmonastery.com
Email: sisters@holyassumptionmonastery.com

The Annunciation
from *The Twelve Great Feasts for Children*

by Mother Melania **Illustrations by Bonnie Gillis**
(first published under her former name – Sister Elayne)

HOLY ASSUMPTION MONASTERY
Calistoga, California

THE TWELVE GREAT FEASTS FOR CHILDREN series:

In the Orthodox Church Year, the Feast of Feasts, in a class by itself, is the Resurrection. After the Resurrection in importance come the twelve Great Feasts. These feasts are the Church's celebration of, and participation in, key events leading to our salvation. The Great Feasts are often separated into Feasts of the Lord and Feasts of the Theotokos.

Feasts of the Lord
Exaltation of the Cross
Nativity of Our Lord (Christmas)
Theophany of Our Lord (Epiphany)
Entry of Our Lord into Jerusalem (Palm Sunday)
Ascension of Our Lord
Pentecost
Transfiguration of Our Lord

Feasts of the Theotokos
Nativity of the Theotokos
Entry of the Theotokos into the Temple
Meeting of Our Lord*
    (Presentation of Christ in the Temple)
Annunciation
Dormition of the Theotokos

* The Meeting of Our Lord is also considered a Feast of the Lord

A final note - Theotokos, an ancient title for the Virgin Mary, means "birthgiver of God." Used since at least the third century, this title guards the truth that Mary's Son is not only fully human, but fully God.

The Feast of the Annunciation is celebrated on March 25

Today is the beginning of our salvation,
the revelation of the eternal mystery!
The Son of God becometh the Son of the Virgin
as Gabriel announceth the coming of grace.
Together with him let us cry to the Theotokos:
Rejoice, O Full of Grace, the Lord is with thee.

-Troparion of the Feast of the Annunciation

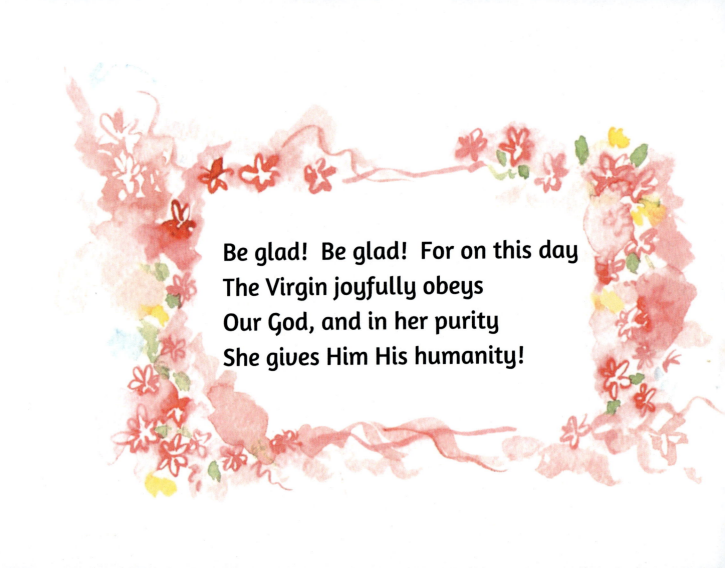

Be glad! Be glad! For on this day
The Virgin joyfully obeys
Our God, and in her purity
She gives Him His humanity!

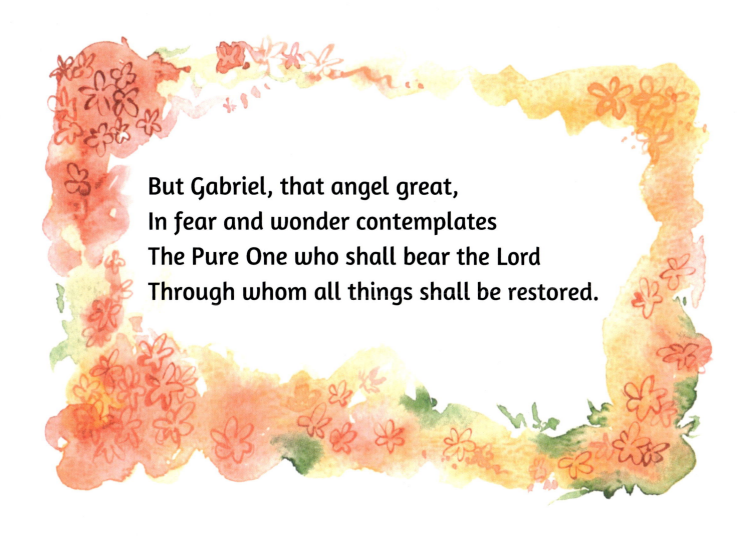

But Gabriel, that angel great,
In fear and wonder contemplates
The Pure One who shall bear the Lord
Through whom all things shall be restored.

So with a glad, but trembling voice,
He tells the Virgin Maid, "Rejoice!
O Full of Grace, through whom the light
Of God shall brighten sin's dark night.

"And as the bush once shone with flame,
Much more, O Lady free from blame,
Shalt thou with Light from heaven shine,
For Thou shalt bear a Son Divine.

"Yes! Thou, O Lady, thou alone,
Art fit to bear this Light, who shone
Before the world and time began,
But now, in love, becomes a Man!"

But she replies, "How can this be—
That I in my virginity
Shall bear the High and Holy One?
How can my God become my Son?"

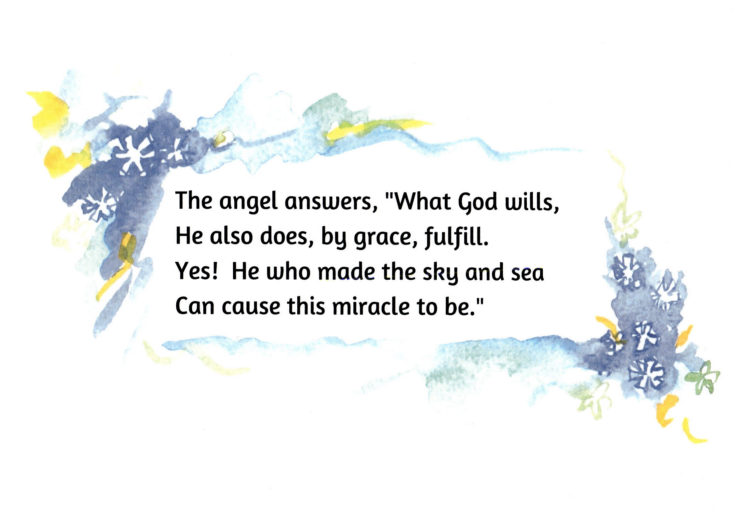

The angel answers, "What God wills,
He also does, by grace, fulfill.
Yes! He who made the sky and sea
Can cause this miracle to be."

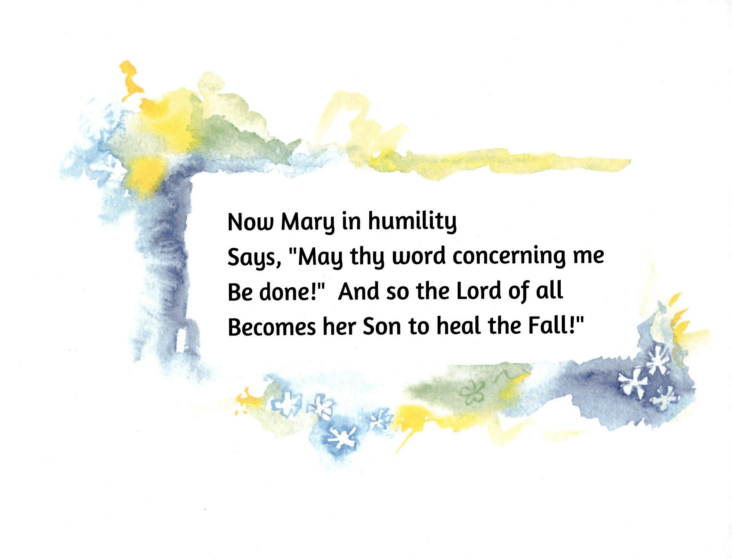

Now Mary in humility
Says, "May thy word concerning me
Be done!" And so the Lord of all
Becomes her Son to heal the Fall!"

Then with a joyful heart, she sings,
"My soul is glad in God my King
And Savior, who has come to seek
The lost and raise up all the meek."

"And with my arms shall I enfold
The One whom heaven cannot hold!
For by a wondrous Virgin Birth
The Lord of lords shall come to earth!"

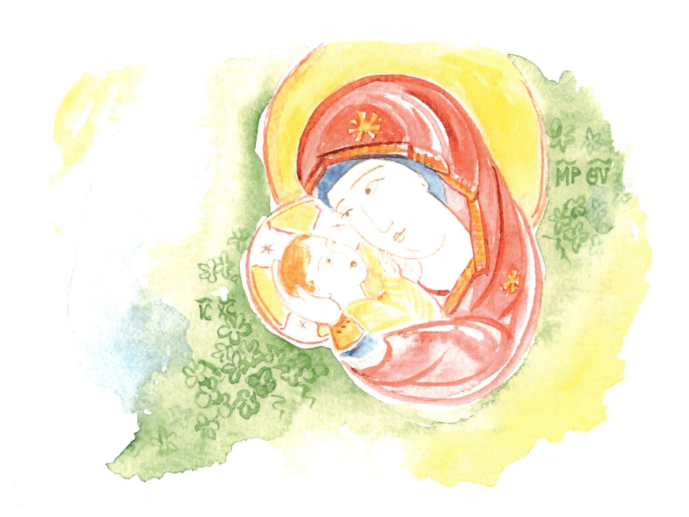

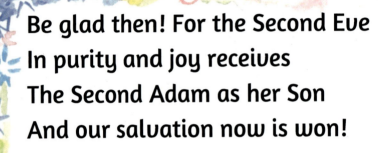

Be glad then! For the Second Eve
In purity and joy receives
The Second Adam as her Son
And our salvation now is won!

Be glad! Be glad! For she shall bear
The King of kings, who comes to share
Our weakness and becomes our cure.
So, let us praise the Virgin pure!

Check out more of Mother Melania's books at
amazon.com/author/mothermelania

 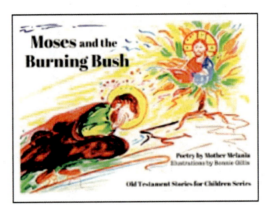 

Mimi the Mynah from **The Fearless & Friends series**

Moses and the Burning Bush from **Old Testament Stories for Children**

Scooter Gets the Point from **The Adventures of Kenny & Scooter**

Please leave a review of this book on Amazon—

BIT.LY/REVIEW-ANNUNCIATION

we're always looking for feedback and ways to improve!

Thanks so much, and God bless you!

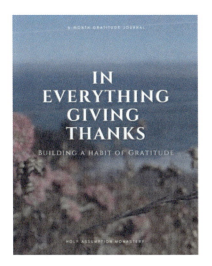

AND PLEASE CHECK OUT OUR MONASTERY'S NEW LINE OF JOURNALS AT

AMAZON.COM/AUTHOR/ HOLYASSUMPTIONMONASTERY

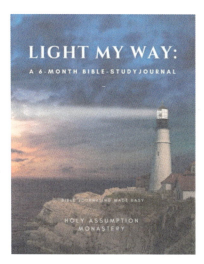

ABOUT THE AUTHOR AND ILLUSTRATOR

Mother Melania is the abbess of Holy Assumption Monastery in Calistoga, California. She has enjoyed working with children all of her life. In addition to The Three-Day Pascha series, she has written several other series of children's books, focusing on Scriptural stories and Great Feasts of the Church, and celebrating the virtues.

Bonnie Gillis is an iconographer and illustrator. She lives in Langley, British Columbia, Canada, where her husband, Father Michael, is pastor of Holy Nativity Orthodox Church.

Made in the USA
Middletown, DE
17 January 2025